STOURBRI
GLASS MU

how it came into being

Graham Fisher MBE FRGS

Trustee, British Glass Foundation

with a foreword by

Lynn Boleyn MBE

Business Manager & Secretary
British Glass Foundation

SPARROW PUBLISHING

BRITISH GLASS
FOUNDATION

First published in UK by Sparrow Publishing 2023 on behalf of the British Glass Foundation
Drovers Barn
Whitney-on-Wye
Herefordshire HR3 6EU

ISBN 978-1-7399212-2-4

Printed and bound in UK by print2demand.co.uk

Cover:
Glass plaque signed by HRH The Duke of Gloucester
at the official opening of Stourbridge Glass Museum
Photo: Allister Malcolm

Dedication

Stourbridge Glass Museum how it came into being is my first foray back into books following the grievous loss of my dear ol' mom Mrs Chipmunk, as Sheila was affectionately known, in November 2022. Always with me, she still is. Which is lovely. Fortunately, I continue to be blessed beyond measure in sharing my life with Mary, my publisher, who has willingly assumed the mantle of thinking I am good *all* of the time. Which is also lovely, especially as 'tis she who magically transforms my sows ears into silk purses.

This one is for both of them, though I am darned sure they each deserve so much more.

Note to self; must try harder.

The author

Graham Fisher is a writer and presenter who has over a lifetime's dedication become a leading authority on the UK's inland waterways, particularly those around the English Midlands. A devoted son of the Black Country, his diverse output has helped him carve a unique niche as an astute observer of the lateral and the arcane. He has been recognized with numerous accolades including MBE (2001), Inland Waterways Personality of the Year (2005) and Fellow of the Royal Geographical Society (2021). He has served on advisory and Governmental bodies, notably as an inaugural appointee to the Canal & River Trust in 2012 where he fulfilled an extended term with distinction. He has many media appearances to his credit and produces his own independent radio broadcasts.

His explorations of links between the Stourbridge Canal and the local glass industry led to his association with the fledgling British Glass Foundation, a body committed to securing a permanent new home for the world-renowned Stourbridge Glass collection. He undertook *ad hoc* PR & Comms from 2009, becoming a Trustee in 2013. In 2015 he sat on the Jury panel of the International Festival of Glass Biennale held in Stourbridge.

In 2013 Graham relocated to the Welsh borders where he lives in a secluded, restored 14th century oak barn with his publisher surrounded by cats, dogs and various other multi-legged critters.

By the same author:

Made in Stourbridge (Sparrow Publishing 2022)
In My Opinion (Sparrow Publishing 2021)
Tales from the Barn (Sparrow Publishing 2019)
Jewels on the Cut (2nd edition) (Sparrow Publishing 2017)
Whiskers on Kittens (Sparrow Publishing 2015)
GlassCuts@50 (Sparrow Publishing 2014)
In Our Time (Sparrow Publishing 2013)
The 2012 Portland Vase Project (Sparrow Publishing 2012)
Jewels on the Cut (1st edition) (Sparrow Publishing 2010)
Playing the Game (Sparrow Publishing 2010)
Out of the Chair (Sparrow Publishing, 2009)
The Sweet Life (Sparrow Publishing, 2004)

Foreword

In the early days against all the odds, the difficulties and the frustrations they faced, the Trustees of the British Glass Foundation, under the leadership of Graham Knowles, have given a new home to the world-renowned Stourbridge glass collection, securing its legacy for generations to come. If they had not persevered the collection may well have remained in storage, never to see the light of day again.

This book not only tells the story of that incredible journey but also serves as a reminder of what the site looked like back in 2015. This has now been transformed from an eyesore in the community into the world-class museum you see today. The Trustees should, rightly, be very proud of what they have achieved, turning a derelict almost burnt-out site into something everyone can be proud of.

The important 400 year history of Stourbridge Glass is detailed so well in this book and reveals the commitment and dedication of the Trustees, and indeed everyone who helped make this dream a reality. From the launch of the charity in 2010 to the formal opening of Stourbridge Glass Museum by HRH The Duke of Gloucester in 2023 this has certainly been history in the making and grateful thanks go to Graham Fisher for documenting this so superbly in his own unique way.

Lynn Boleyn
Business Manager and Secretary
British Glass Foundation

Notes:

Much of the information related herein is based on contemporaneous notes and reportage compiled since 2009 and is reproduced here in edited form. Subsequent additions will be self-evident.

Reference is made to 'the new White House Cone museum of glass', a dated nomenclature that served its purpose for a time. Under professional re-branding the facility became known as **Stourbridge Glass Museum**. It is the same building; only the name changed as part of corporate consolidation.

ERDF refers to the European Regional Development Fund.

HLF refers to the earlier Heritage Lottery Fund, now known as the National Lottery Heritage Fund (**NLHF**) since its rebranding in January 2019.

Both **ERDF** and **NLHF** are principal sponsors of Stourbidge Glass Museum.

Images in this book are courtesy of the British Glass Foundation and the Stourbridge Glass Museum except those annotated 'SB' which are by Simon Bruntnell.

www.britishglassfoundation.org.uk

Contents

What it's all about . . . . pg 8

Becoming the British Glass Foundation . . . . pg 9

BGF to SGM timeline . . . . pg 17

Publications . . . . pg 21

Promotion and fundraising . . . . pg 23

Supporters and sponsors . . . . pg 35

Ruin to rebirth . . . . pg 37

Onwards and upwards . . . . pg 49

Epilogue . . . . pg 56

What it's all about

You'll never do it.
We heard this many times. From many different people. They are already confined to yesterday. But, I confess, there were occasions we even thought it ourselves. *Against The Odds* (an early working title for this book) is often how it felt.

The 'it', of course, refers to the new Stourbridge Glass Museum (SGM). The 'we' was a group of wildly disparate individuals who through rare fate were brought together by a common cause to form the British Glass Foundation (BGF). To suggest the creation of Stourbridge Glass Museum irrevocably changed all of our lives is no hyperbole; in the classical sense it came close to driving some of us quite mad. But in a spirit of determined cooperation and mutual respect between partners that may prove a model for future projects, we did it.

The tangible results of the BGF's efforts can now be seen a'nestling in Wordsley in the West Midlands at the heart of the world-famous Glass Quarter. A 'People's Museum' in which the support of the populace was deemed crucial to its success. And all achieved, from raw aspiration to concrete reality capped with an official Royal opening, in a tad under thirteen years. Within the landscape of such ventures, this timeline *per se* is extraordinary

From the day Stourbridge Glass Museum threw its doors to the public in April 2022, followed by an official opening in April 2023, it offered a beacon of excellence reflecting the area's immense contribution over more than four centuries to the narrative of glass. The rest, as they say, is history. Or at least will become so as the years unfurl; and the reference point for the continuance of this narrative will forever be defined by a direct line back to that opening.

But how did we actually arrive here? What brought us together in the first instance? What drove us for nigh-on thirteen years in pursuit of this beautiful madness? Quite simply, just what is the back-story of the entire enterprise before it finally took physical form in bricks and mortar? These, and many more, are questions to which historians of the future probing the roots of the museum's *raison d'être* will seek answers.

This first-hand account, always the best source of primary evidence, from someone who was there from the outset – and who, at the time of writing, is one of only a handful of the original cohort remaining *in situ* – will save tomorrow's researchers a whole bundle of trouble. It is also in its own right no less a stirring and inspirational narrative of success. It was consistently hard work, it was inevitably frustrating, it was forever demanding and things didn't always go to plan. Oh, no. But above all, it was immensely enjoyable. My goodness, did we share some laughter along the way.

So, if you are sitting comfortably and of a disposition to hear how we defied the gainsayers, then I'll tell you a tale …

Graham Fisher
November 2023

Acknowledgements are noted throughout the text but I would like to record my particular appreciation to Graham Knowles, BGF Chairman; Lynn Boleyn MBE, BGF Business Manager & Secretary and Allister Malcolm, Resident Glassmaker at SGM in the compilation of this work.

Stourbridge Glass

The Stourbridge Glass collection is without question one of the most important of its type in the world and deserves a permanent home that is appropriate, sustainable and fit for purpose in the long term.

The Stourbridge Glass Quarter in this context is centred on Stourbridge and the surrounding area and includes the former Broadfield House Glass Museum, Red House Glass Cone (formerly Stuart), Ruskin Glass Centre (formerly Webb Corbett/ Royal Doulton), various factories and studios plus numerous retail outlets and entrepreneurs operating in all aspects of glassmaking and decoration. The glass collection represents one of the finest holdings of British 18th, 19th and 20th century glass in the world and includes stunning examples from every major period of glass production in this country. The highlight of the collection is cameo glass, the speciality of Stourbridge factories at the end of the 19th century.

The collection also includes essential glass archive material such as pattern books from Stevens & Williams, Richardson's and Thomas Webb & Sons, together with two major glass libraries from Robert J. Charleston, former Curator at the Victoria & Albert Museum, and H. Jack Haden, a local historian who amassed a valuable collection of Stourbridge material.

The glass library is one of the finest in the country and includes the complete microfiche catalogue of original glass catalogues owned by the Corning Museum of Glass in America, the only museum in this country to own this valuable research facility. Notable archive pieces include the only surviving 'Pull-Up' machine invented by John Northwood 1st in the 1880s to decorate glassware at Stevens & Williams, and a rare complete example of a Bohemian copper-wheel engraving lathe which was used by the legendary Joseph Keller.

Another item of historical significance is the remains of a 16th century glassworks that were unearthed in 1991-2 during a site excavation on the estate of Sir Charles Wolseley near Rugeley in Staffordshire. Three furnaces were found, with Furnace 1 being particularly well preserved.

The furnaces would have made white crown window glass, possibly as early as the 1540s. Restrictions on the use of wood as fuel after 1615 in the UK diverted manufacture towards the coalfields of Newcastle and Stourbridge. The fuel would probably have fed the furnace along the brick flue visible in the photograph.

The remains are in the custody of Stourbridge Glass Museum awaiting interpretation.

Furnace 1 in situ at Rugeley before excavation

So, let us hop aboard our time machine and travel back to a chilly evening in early 2009. The location is Wordsley Community Hall near Stourbridge where the walls were close to bulging with attendees. Including me, here in my capacity as a broadcaster with a nearby radio station eager to be the first with the reportage.

At the head table was an assemblage of various officials, Councillors and representatives of Dudley MBC. Their thankless mission was to explain the proposed closure of nearby Broadfield House Glass

Museum, home of the Stourbridge Glass collection. Dudley Council had announced closure plans to the staff at Broadfield House Glass Museum on the 5th January 2009. The later public meeting at Wordsley can be most charitably described as 'tetchy' and I did not envy their task one iota.

I will leave the finer details to our future chroniclers but in essence the problem was that in a time of austerity the Council were obliged to curtail costs. In simple terms the offending costs were matched by expenditures at the museum. *Et voilà,* close the museum. Sorted.

Broadfield House Glass Museum

Except …

Two facts became apparent during that meeting.

Firstly, many of the representatives did not fully realise the significance of the collection housed in Broadfield House.

Secondly, there was an under-recognition of the affection in which the collection, and indeed the house, were held. Nevertheless, and with acknowledgement for the dilemma in which the council found itself, the closure was to go ahead.

The fall-out was immediate and within a short time the whole gamut from media exposure to support groups was mobilised. An early example of the latter was the **Save Our Glass Heritage** campaign formed on 18th March 2009 by a group of concerned locals following international outcry at the closure proposals. Though enthusiastic and active the group's scope was limited; something more cohesive and focused was required. The central issue was the fate of the **collection** – note the word. The individual items could be placed in storage anywhere for safe keeping but, quite apart from the fact they might not be accessible to the public, there is the integrity of the collection itself. Should it be broken down as individual items and stored in separate locations then it would lose its provenance as a collated representation of some of the finest glassware ever made. It simply had to have a new home.

Thus it was that a few weeks later I attended a packed meeting at Stream Road Methodist Church Hall in Kingswinford where local businessman, philanthropist and glass enthusiast Graham Knowles (much of the cameo on display at Broadfield House emanated from his family) headed a table together with Secretary Lynn Boleyn.

The group needed support and I felt enthused to offer it, particularly in light of my developing examination of the local canals and the industries, notably glass, that they served. So, immediately following the meeting I submitted proposals for a media campaign and mechanisms for disseminating information. These were taken on board and I was invited by Graham Knowles, Chairman of the fledgling group, to pursue the role. Thus did I became *de facto* Public Relations and Communications for the British Glass Foundation, being subsequently appointed as a Trustee alongside glassmaker Allister Malcolm, formerly resident glassmaker at Broadfield House Glass Museum, in January 2013.

The launch of the British Glass Foundation at Hagley Hall in November 2010

The BGF was initiated on 30th March 2010 and formally launched in the splendid surroundings of Hagley Hall, near Stourbridge on 24th November 2010 with many celebrities from the world of glass attending. This was done with backing from numerous organisations including Friends of Broadfield House Glass Museum, The Glass Association and The Glass Circle (later to both merge as The Glass Society), Scottish Glass Society, Contemporary Glass Society, Glass Collaborations and the British Society of Scientific Glassblowers, to name but some.

The British Glass Foundation

• seeks to represent all other charities, organisations and individuals that have an interest in preserving our glass heritage.

• continues to raise the profile of the importance, locally, nationally and internationally, of the Dudley glass collections and archives.

• works closely in partnership with Dudley Council, the principal custodian of the glass collections, to accomplish its objectives.

• will promote contemporary glass artists.

The British Glass Foundation is an enabling body bringing together all relevant and independent glass and cultural organisations and private individuals, in our common aim to protect and save the glass, archive and technical collections previously held at Broadfield House Glass Museum, and to ensure their future display to the public, access for research and continued growth.

The early weeks of the BGF saw a state of flux as participants came or departed but eventually the line-up settled to an eclectic group with hitherto nothing in common save the English language and a passion for glass, Stourbridge Glass in particular.

With a lifetime's experience of business the aforementioned Graham Knowles was a natural choice as Chair; he was supported by recruitment consultant Meriel Harris and past Chair & CEO of the legendary Stevens & Williams (later Royal Brierley) David Williams-Thomas DL. A core member of the team was Lynn Boleyn (later to be ennobled with an MBE for services outside of glass) who was ultimately to become Business Manager and personal PA to the Chair.

Graham Knowles   Meriel Harris   David Williams-Thomas

Graham Fisher   Allister Malcolm   Lynn Boleyn

Over the ensuing years we recruited a further tranche of appointees to expand the breadth of experience across the board.

So, at October 2021, the 'driving force' of Trustees behind the BGF comprised;
   David Williams-Thomas DL (former Trustee and then Patron)
   Graham Knowles (Chairman)
   Allister Malcolm (Glassmaker)
   Graham Fisher (PR & Communications)
   Meriel Harris (Treasurer)
   Greg Cook (Museums specialist)
   Gavin Whitehouse (Accountant)
   Prof James Measell (USA-based historian and scholar)
   Will Farmer (Auctioneer and TV Presenter)
   Dr Audrey Whitty (Museums specialist based in Ireland)
   Lynn Boleyn (Business Manager & Secretary)

together with independent Advisers and Ambassadors;
   John Hughes (ex-Black Country Living Museum)
   Viv Astling OBE (ex-Chief Executive Dudley MBC)
   Charles Hajdamach (glass expert, author and former Trustee).

Since that time in 2021 Finance man Phil Cook touched down with us briefly before retiring due to ill health; glass expert John Smith became a Trustee before ill health also took its toll. Greg Cook and Meriel Harris (2022) and Dr Audrey Whitty (2023) resigned as Trustees but we were joined in 2022 by Chris Day (Glassmaker), Elliot Walker (Glassmaker) and Larry Priest (BPN Architects).

From 2020 management operations were delegated to a team of professional specialists; a Museum Director was initially appointed but the role was redesignated as Museum Manager when Alexander Goodger joined us in October 2022.

The day-to-day running of the museum is supported by a wonderfully enthusiastic ensemble of volunteers, some of whom continued from the Broadfield House days but with numerous fresh faces, too.

Early days

Those early days were challenging, the biggest issue being BGF's credibility. From the outset BGF was determined to be seen as apolitical (hence no comment on the politics behind the closure of Broadfield House), independent and entirely philanthropic. It's problem as a new group was a lack of track record or provenance. Hardly surprising, but what to do?

I would contend that our greatest single achievement of the time was a concerted campaign to generate credibility and within a few months we were sitting at the top table with the decision-makers. Having established our *bona fides* we went on to attract the affections of other groups and individuals such that we became – entirely unintentionally but we embraced it with open arms – an umbrella organisation representing their collective interests.

We also recognised the universal potential for promoting the history of glass, highlighting its contemporary practitioners and supporting the vision of glassmaking into a sustainable future. This, by any yardstick, was a world advanced from our initial objectives but we accepted the role.

Webb Corbett glass workers from the 1950s
Ernie Franks, left, glass blower
Frank Ostin, below, glass maker

Public support

Another priority was public support; we knew we would get nowhere without it. Key to achieving this was building our relationships across the media and in our promise to keep everyone informed of developments at the earliest. Thus, *inter alia* and in addition to regular press releases, was born our email bulletin *GlassCuts*. An initial foray with an accompanying newsletter was quickly discontinued as superfluous and *GlassCuts* was destined to become 'The Journal of the British Glass Foundation; the Voice of Stourbridge Glass Museum' in an email bulletin that now attracts contributions and readership worldwide; we know this from correspondence and submissions received. The glossy printed newsletter lasted for just five issues; they are by now probably collectors' items.

What next?

So, having established our credentials, where now? The need for a new museum, especially designated and ideally situated within the Glass Quarter, was paramount. The site of Stuart Crystal in Wordsley, derelict since 2001 when it closed with the loss of 220 jobs, seemed ideal so we negotiated with the owners Complex Development Projects Ltd, who were enthused by the idea. This was the perfect plot and was our Plan A. Truth is, we discussed several back-up ideas, one of which included the wholly impractical notion of attempting something with Broadfield House (hardly likely but we were determined) yet we promoted Plan A alone so as not to create the impression that we were ever seriously considering anything else. The Stuart site it was.

The derelict White House Cone site in Wordsley

Iconic building

It was an especially significant attainment in securing such an iconic building that until quite recently housed a major player right in the heart of the Stourbridge Glass industry. Stuart was the last 'serious heavyweight' in the quarter to go and was distinguished by many attainments, not least in supplying glasses and decanters for the White Star Line, owners of the ill-fated *RMS Titanic*. The company was legendary and held in high regard by both employees and locals alike, providing not only a source of work but a focus of pride, and its loss was keenly felt.

The truncated White House glass cone and Red House across the road

The resurgence of the site as a world-class museum accentuating this heritage could only add to the kudos. The intention from the outset was therefore a long-game meld of historical attainment coupled with a promotion of the contemporary local glass scene combining in a sum greater than their individual parts in inspiring glassmaking and its practitioners for the future. It merits an entire tale in itself and our future historians will find much to evaluate beyond this simply being a practical location for a museum.

Spiritually, emotionally, almost sacredly; it just had to be here.

Stuart Crystal in 1967: The cone had its top removed in 1939 and was completely demolished in 1979.

Funding

Thus began the painstaking process of securing funding and, in encapsulating endless months of effort within a few words, it is a long, long process. The ERDF granted the finance to convert the building, quickly followed by NHLF funding to complete the fit-out. Great stuff, but even so we had to endure many more months of hoop-jumping to clear all of the monies. Yet still the donations came in; from big-time philanthropists to dedicated individuals sending us a few bob, we attracted them all. And every single one, irrespective of the amount, is equally appreciated for the support it represents.

Fundraising never stops; there is always the need for an ongoing revenue stream. Which begs the question as to why people should be moved to support us. We believe we found the answer, which lay in our single-minded determination to create a 'People's Museum' where elitism would hold no sway; a facility where the good people of Stourbridge and beyond could equally share in their heritage and help forge its continuance in a celebration of both what was and what is yet to come.

Having a defined aspiration, rather than a nebulous intent, tends to focus the mind and our supporters rallied to the cause magnificently. It should be recorded here that the venture always has been entirely philanthropic; no Trustee receives a penny-piece for the efforts and all monies raised go to 'the cause'.

Registered charity

The BGF is now widely recognised for its integrity and breadth of intellect, being the only party that could accept custody of the collections, and working closely with Dudley Council and Complex Development Projects Ltd. Both the site and the glass collection are entrusted to BGF on a 125-year lease arrangement.

The BGF also works very closely with the other major tourist attractions in the area, e.g. Dudley Zoo and Castle, Black Country Living Museum, Wrens Nest Nature Reserve, Canal & River Trust, the Glass Quarter, Ruskin Glass Centre, Red House Cone and also the major hotel chains. It is keen to link together and to highlight all the attractions and so draw visitors to the area to help boost tourism in Dudley and the local economy.

Connections

The Charity has very close connections and relationships with Corning Museum of Glass NY, the British Museum and the Victoria & Albert Museum in London. Following the designation of UNESCO Dudley Global Geopark status in July 2020, since its opening the new museum is now included as one of the Geosites within the Geopark.

The Dudley limestone caverns Geosite

BGF to SGM timeline

Raising the funds

January 2011
An outline ERDF application was put together by Complex Development Projects Ltd (CDP) for Dudley Council in conjunction with the BGF for the funding of a new museum on the derelict White House Cone site in Wordsley opposite the Red House Cone.

8th September 2011
The Museum of Glass book was produced detailing the plans for the new museum on the site.

14th September 2011
A Memorandum of Understanding between the BGF and Dudley Council was signed, cementing the relationship between the Charity and the Council.

February 2012
It was suggested by Dudley Council to include the Red House Cone site in the ERDF funding application and the intention was to join the two sites together *via* an underground tunnel. However, this did not go ahead and discussions were then held for a 'scaled back' version to include workshops/office accommodation to provide rental income towards the running of the new museum.

28th February 2013
An outline ERDF application for £2,147,844 was successful and a full application was invited.

17th April 2013
A meeting was held with Dudley Council to discuss the BGF becoming a Museum Trust to take over the glass collections and legal agreements were drawn up.

March 2014
Funding from Growing Places was applied for and approved. This was for a grant of £645,699 to cover the purchase price of the offices (allowing the Council to acquire these from CDP and then gift them to the BGF) and also a Growing Places Loan of £400,000. This was originally intended to be a grant to cover any shortfall on the sale of Broadfield House Glass Museum but is confirmed only as a loan leaving Dudley Council/BGF to make up the shortfall if any. The loan was intended to part-pay CDP during the construction of the building.

May 2014
The BGF was successful with its My Community Rights Pre-Feasibility grant application for £10,000 towards its legal and accountancy costs to set up the Museum Trust.

10th July 2014
Formal approval was received for ERDF funding and in September 2014 we were successful with a Heritage Lottery Start Up grant application of £10,000 to cover research, consultation and to update the BGF's website. A robust Business Plan was also drawn up.

21st October 2014
Planning approval was given by Dudley Council for the building of the new museum on the White House Cone site. The Planning Committee Chairman said: *This application ticks all the boxes. It is a welcome development that will bring together residential, a visitor attraction and a boost to the local economy.*

24th October 2014
A meeting was held with Margot James MP for Stourbridge to update her on progress. She agreed to provide a letter to Heritage Lottery supporting our application for funding stressing the importance of this project for the local community and for our heritage.

16th February 2015
Demolition work started on the White House Cone site in preparation for building work to start when ERDF was formally signed off. Steady as she goes – all making good progress. Then . . .

23rd March 2020
The Prime Minster announced the first UK national lockdown – the Covid-19 pandemic.
Everything was on hold but much was still going on behind the scenes to keep us on track.

Friday 23rd July 2021
Our 'Big Announcement' via a special supplement to *GlassCuts 183* and the media. This was probably one of the most significant markers in BGF's history in which we announced:
- A complete rebranding of the museum 'to create a robust profile for the museum that will translate positively into developing its public perception for the longer term'. The facility formerly referred to as White House Cone museum of glass will henceforth be known and marketed as Stourbridge Glass Museum.
  Its mission statement is: *Stourbridge Glass Museum: at the heart of the community with a globally significant collection to educate and inspire.*
- The launch of a vibrant new website **www.stourbridgeglassmuseum.org.uk**
- And, crucially, a confirmed date for the Grand Opening on 9th April 2022.

Comprehensively populated before launch, the website is added to and updated regularly. Initially the site included:
a brief history of the Stourbridge Glass collection
other history, including a 'from then to now of the BGF and the Stuart Crystal site'
latest news from the world of glass
exhibitions and galleries
dates of forthcoming shows, presentations and events and how to become involved
special notices
education and learning resources
latest news from our hot-glass studio, including demonstrations and 'hands-on' sessions
admission details
volunteers, and how to become one
directions to our home
repository for our publications
… plus much, much more. The sky really is the limit with this one.

9th April 2022

2022 was a serendipitous year in creating a perfect storm in the world of glass, being the same year as;

- the International Festival of Glass, based in Stourbridge and including the new museum,
- the 25th anniversary of one of our key supporters the Contemporary Glass Society,
- becoming an incorporated member of the recently-formed UNESCO Global Geopark,
- the United Nations designation as the International Year of Glass (IYOG).

We were delighted to note that the IYOG Newsletter for Great Britain and Ireland, Edition 4, dated 2nd December 2021 cited the opening of Stourbridge Glass Museum. This was a most welcome recognition of our efforts on a grand - *international* - scale, of which we were understandably proud. However, the year proved to be especially memorable for us, with the 'soft' opening of a world-class museum housing one of the most revered collections of Stourbridge Glass right at the heart of it.

Media support

From the beginning our media drive was extensive in scope but we never lost sight of relationships with our all-important local support base, without whose support we probably would not have laid a single brick. Ongoing progress was disseminated regularly through electronic bulletins, social media and traditional print – principal amongst these being *Express & Star* and their *Chronicles* range, *Black Country Bugle* and *Stourbridge News*. We are particularly grateful to the latter, and their Chief Reporter Bev Holder, who has been fully engaged with the project from the start.

Similarly ***Village Voice***, founded by the late Chris Smith and now produced by his wife Gail, is a delightful little monthly magazine that focuses locally to the extent that it is produced in three different content-formats to accommodate differing areas of the southern Black Country. It doesn't get much more 'local' than that.

Examples of the *Village Voice* contributions

The Blackcountryman – 'The Black Country's Premier Heritage Magazine', a quarterly publication of the eponymous society, carried an illustrated three-page spread in its Winter 2021 edition detailing the *(then)* current status at Stourbridge Glass Museum. In the Summer 2022 edition we were afforded a seven-page feature – by any yardstick tremendous coverage and support.

In December 2021, *Art Quarterly*, the official magazine of the Art Fund, requested an article for their March 2022 edition outlining the history of Stourbridge Glass and the creation of Stourbridge Glass Museum. The feature provided by Graham Fisher included details of the glass collection as well as the 2012 Portland Vase Project and the Eila Grahame collection, a bequest of 136 glass objects acquired for Dudley Museums Service with Art Fund support that would feature in the displays.

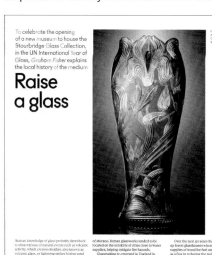

BGF publications

GlassCuts

'The journal of the British Glass Foundation', later to become 'the voice of Stourbridge Glass Museum'. An occasional email bulletin, *GlassCuts* was always intended to focus on the glass world in general but Stourbridge in particular, and especially on the efforts of BGF to find a new home for the Stourbridge collection. Contributions on just about anything to do with glass and those who make, decorate, sell, repair or in any other legitimate manner are involved in it, were welcome. However, as our Chairman Graham Knowles points out: *it will offer future generations a glimpse of what was going on in the world of glass in the early part of the 21st century and thus will become an important archival document.*

Newsletter

Originally there were plans for a formal quarterly Newsletter with the informal *GlassCuts* providing a brief intermediate update of snippets – especially news items and matters pertaining to the Museum proposals – that were too late for one Newsletter but which couldn't wait for the next. It was thought that a bulletin of a couple of pages or so issued three or four times *per annum* in between Newsletters would be just the ticket. However, *GlassCuts* is typically between six and ten pages issued every two weeks. Its frequency has effectively negated the requirement for a regular Newsletter, the last edition of which was Number 5 of March 2013.

Museum of Glass

Museum of Glass

Created by Bryant Priest Newman, a book illustrating the vision for creating the new museum.

GlassCuts@50

A limited edition book of highlights from the first 50 issues of *GlassCuts* compiled by Graham Fisher.

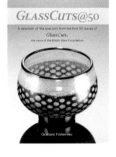

GLASSCUTS@50

BGF has produced many booklets, brochures, flyers, leaflets and the like, promoting what's going on behind the scenes and advertising events, presentations, glass demonstrations, personal appearances and lectures – all with the aim of raising public awareness and funds for the BGF.

Other publications

BGF Trustee, Graham Fisher, has written several books on Stourbridge Glass and produced *The Crystal Mile - Along The Stourbridge Canal* an enchanting DVD that explores the heart of glassmaking and other industries from the perspective of a walk along the Stourbridge Canal.

His books on glass include:

The 2012 Portland Vase Project – Recreation of a Masterpiece with a foreword by the late David Whitehouse, Senior Scholar, Corning Museum of Glass NY;

In Our Time an appreciation of Stourbridge Glass and a review of the 2012 Portland Vase Project;

Whiskers on Kittens a celebratory romp through the Stourbridge Glass Industry; and

Jewels on the Cut an exploration of the Stourbridge Canal and the local glass industry with an extensively updated second edition, *Jewels on the Cut II*.

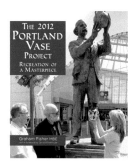  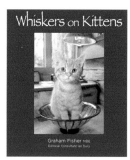 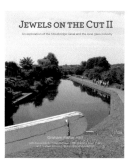

History West Midlands Magazine Spring 2014 issue was dedicated to Glass and Glassmaking and featured articles by

Graham Fisher – *The Stourbridge Glass Industry: then and now*,

Charles Hajdamach – *Stourbridge Glass: a cut above the rest* and

James Measell – *The Stourbridge School of Art: Design Education for Artisans.*

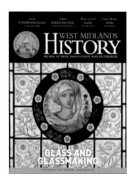

Also from *History West Midlands*;

The rise, fall and renaissance of the glass industry – a podcast where Graham Fisher talks to Charles R Hajdamach, a leading authority on British glass and a Fellow of the Society of Glass Technology.

The Portland Vase – an enigma in glass – a video where Graham Fisher explores the mysteries of the Roman cameo vase, how it triggered the cameo glass movement in Stourbridge in the 19th century and inspired the idea for its recreation in 2012.

Thesis on the Stourbridge School of Art

James Measell, Honorary Research Fellow (University of Birmingham) Awarded the University of Birmingham *Ashley Prize* as 'the highest quality thesis in Economic & Social History within the Schools of History & Cultures, Business, Social Policy or Government & Society.'

Three Centuries of Glass Auction, 9th April 2011

29 Glass Artists and seven private individuals generously donated pieces to be sold in aid of funds to the BGF. Within the overall remit of the BGF to protect and save the glass collections at Broadfield House Glass Museum, one of its aims is to support and promote contemporary glass artists. It was pleasantly ironic, therefore, that it should be a group of glass artists who were among the very first to donate unique examples of their work to help raise much needed funds to allow the BGF to carry out its work.

The Trustees are very grateful to Will Farmer and all the staff at Fieldings Auctioneers Ltd for including these items in what has become the best and most comprehensive annual glass auction in the country where £7,100 was raised for the BGF. Bidders who were successful in acquiring one of the donated pieces will no doubt feel a proud sense of involvement and support for a cause which has touched the hearts of glass collectors and artists around the world. Will Farmer and Eric Knowles, both of Antiques Roadshow fame, who both attended the official launch of the Charity, have been extremely supportive of the BGF where Eric often refers to himself as a Patron of the Charity.

Triple Cased Cameo Vase
by Jonathan Harris

Graal Technique Vase
by Malcolm Andrews

How Does Your
Garden Grow
by Rachel Elliott

Stevens & Williams 1930's Cut Glass Vase
Donated by Dr Graham Cooley

Some of the pieces sold at the glass auction

Charles Hajdamach's visit to Corning Museum of Glass, Corning NY, 21st October 2011

Renowned glass expert and, at the time, a BGF Trustee, Charles R Hajdamach, paid a visit to the world-famous Corning Museum of Glass NY, where he delivered a presentation that was streamed

live on the web – one of only four of the lectures from the entire three day seminar.

Whilst in New York, Charles presented a copy of the BGF book *Museum of Glass* to Karol Wight, the new Executive Director of The Corning Museum of Glass (on the right) and Jane Shadel Spillman, Curator of American Glass, at the 50th anniversary seminar at The Corning Museum of Glass.

Jane Shadel Spillman, Charles
Hajdamach and Karol Wight

Hagley Hall Gala Day, 22 August 2012
From Rome To Stourbridge – 2000 Years of Cameo Glass

Attended by the Mayor and Mayoress of Dudley and David Whitehouse from Corning Museum of Glass NY, this event, at Hagley Hall in Stourbridge, generously supported by the Glass Association and Friends of Broadfield House Glass Museum, was a huge success and a commemoration of cameo glass in which the Stourbridge glass industry has historically excelled.

The event featured talks by renowned speakers, Dr Paul Roberts, then Curator of Roman Art and Archaeology Department at The British Museum, who spoke on Ancient Roman Cameo Glass, and Charles Hajdamach, author and former Trustee of the BGF who spoke on The Glories of Stourbridge Cameo Glass.

To commemorate the 400th anniversary of glassmaking in Stourbridge the 2012 Portland Vase was unveiled by its creators, Richard Golding, Ian Dury and Terri-Louise Colledge.

Ian Dury, Richard Golding, Graham Fisher and Terri-Louise Colledge

The original Portland Vase at The British Museum dates back to AD5 to 25. The team also re-created the historic Auldjo Jug – another important piece of Roman Cameo glass also held at the British Museum – as well as an amphora.

International Festival of Glass, 26th August 2012
World's Longest Glassmaking Demonstration

The 5th International Festival of Glass celebrated 400 years of glassmaking in Stourbridge with glassmakers from around the world sharing their skills. As part of the festival Allister Malcolm, resident glass artist at Broadfield House Glass Museum, went head to head with Elliot Walker, glass artist at Red House Glass Cone in a gruelling endurance test to put on the world's longest glassmaking demonstration raising funds for the BGF.

The Mayor of Dudley, Melvyn Mottram, started off the challenge with a spot of glass blowing, aided by glassmaker Tim Boswell. The community spirit and support was sensational. Around £3,000 was raised from this event itself with additional funds raised at the annual *Decades of Design* sale at Fieldings where these unique items were auctioned on 27th October raising a further £9,830.

The 2012 Portland Vase Project

The original Portland Vase is Roman, lies in the British Museum and is probably one of the most enigmatic pieces of cameo glass the world has ever seen. The vase was spectacularly recreated not once, but twice, in the 19th century, by Stourbridge craftsmen. There is a connection here for inland waterways fans; they were made within yards of each other, on opposite sides of the road that goes over the Stourbridge Canal Main Line at Wordsley. Both the Richardson-Locke attempt (which was uncompleted; the figures weren't finished) and the Northwood-Pargeter effort housed in the Corning Museum of Glass, Corning NY. There were a couple of further recreations in the 20th century, notably the amphora interpretation of 1990 by Steve Bradley who completed the entire process himself, from blowing the blank to effecting the decoration and making a stand. There is also the 1987 undertaking by Josef Welzel who reproduced an amphora with lid.

Ian Dury announced in 2011 his proposals to recreate the Portland Vase with the intention of demonstrating that Stourbridge still has the skills within its ranks, and to lay to rest the myth that the Stourbridge Glass industry is dead. Supported by numerous artisans and back-room enthusiasts, all sharing the same passion, the aspirations of 2011 became the realities of 2012 when, on that incredible day in September, glassmaker Richard Golding blew the blanks upon which Terri-Louise Colledge was then let loose to weave her magic.

The team produced a total of four flat-bottomed vases, one amphora and an Auldjo Jug, this last piece being a possible precursor to the original Portland Vase. Of these, one flat-bottomed vase, the amphora, and the Auldjo Jug were engraved, together with a replica base disc. A 'spoilt' vase was to be carved with Greco-Roman sporting figures, in recognition of 2012 being London Olympics year.

The Auldjo Jug was first to be fully completed, quickly followed by the flat-bottomed Portland Vase. They were officially displayed to the public at Hagley Hall on 22nd August 2012

The story of this momentous achievement is recorded in the official biography *The 2012 Portland Vase Project; Recreation of a Masterpiece* by Graham Fisher MBE and in the more recent 2023 leaflet *Made in Stourbridge* that describes the project in a compact format.

On Saturday 24th September 2013 almost exactly a year since the official launch of the Portland Vase and the Auldjo Jug, Terri Colledge informed us that she had finished the last vestiges of carving on the final piece in the jigsaw, the amphora version of the Portland Vase.

It is also worth recording for posterity that, assuming the original Portland Vase was engraved by a man (a wholly reasonable assumption), and knowing the provenance of all the others, this represents the first time in history that a Portland Vase of any description has been fashioned by female hands.

Ian Dury very kindly offered all these pieces on permanent loan to the BGF to display in the new museum, affording visitors the opportunity to see the entire completed collection under one roof.

The Portland Vase Project items on display in the upper galley of the museum

Parkhead Canal Festival 2012

The BGF supported the Parkhead Canal Festival in 2012 where copies of *Jewels on the Cut* were sold with proceeds to BGF coffers. Canals and glass are, of course, inextricably linked and the BGF are delighted to support the work of Dudley Canal Trust. Graham Fisher is a waterways enthusiast and a former Harbourmaster for previous Parkhead Festivals. He is a qualified skipper and was engaged at the time by Dudley Canal Trust to conduct guided boat trips through the limestone caverns.

Centuries of Glass Auction

A further auction sale was held at Fieldings on 23rd March 2013 which raised £605 for the BGF. Some pieces were kept back for a future sale due to bad weather.

Birmingham Lives History Fair

Graham Fisher had a stall at the above Fair on 9th June 2013 which featured history societies and genealogy groups together with sales of books, postcards and souvenirs. Graham also took along the 2012 Portland Vase pieces.

The author promoting the
BGF at the History Fair

Mayor's Civic Awards 2013

Allister Malcolm, Trustee and resident glass artist at Broadfield House Glass Museum was invited once again to make the pieces for the prestigious annual Dudley MBC Civic Awards.

Each of the six individual awards are named after a local hero and are conferred under the categories of community spirit, environment, sport, arts, education and business.

The Mayor of Dudley, Melvyn Mottram, and Allister
with one of his pieces to be awarded as a prize

A Black Country Experience, July 2013

The 50th Anniversary celebrations of the British Cartographic Society included a weekend of all things Black Country. Starting with a boat trip through the Dudley limestone caverns (captained by Graham Fisher) the first day was followed by a tour of the Black Country Living Museum and a visit to the Dudley Archives where several treasures had been put on display for the visit. Next day a guided canal walk through the Stourbridge Glass Industry concluded with a visit to Red House Cone and a presentation by Graham on the 2012 Portland Vase. And the 2012 vase was there.

Royal Geographical Society - Discovering Britain

The Crystal Canal - A self-guided walk along the stourbridge canal is the latest in the Society's Discovering Britain series *(as at September 2013)* and examines the myriad glassworks and other industries from the perspective of the canal that runs right through it.

Based on Graham Fisher's *Jewels on the Cut* the guide is available as a free audio or PDF download. The PDF can be printed off as a hard copy and Graham has also provided a MP3 voice track so that it can be used as an audio guide. Featured locations include The Bonded Warehouse, Ruskin Glass Centre and Red House Glass Cone. There is also reference to the work of the British Glass Foundation seeking to create a new canalside world-class museum to house the renowned Stourbridge Glass collection. The walk (updated since the second edition of the book) can be downloaded from:
https://www.discoveringbritain.org/activities/west-midlands/walks/stourbridge-canal.html

An Audience with Graham Fisher MBE – More Miles than Venice

A part of outreach beyond the local area, Graham delivered a presentation on the Black Country waterways with an emphasis on glassmaking and the Portland Vase Project at The Rhydspence Inn in Herefordshire on 24th October 2013. *(Repeated regularly at different venues since.)*

Archives Awareness Week

Graham Fisher manned a stand all day at the brand new Dudley Archives Centre on 16th November. Although not fully operational, the centre was opened to the public as part of the Archives Awareness Week. Graham presented the story of the 2012 Portland Vase which was on display on his stand.

The George Woodall Plaque

12th December 2013 saw the unveiling of a rather distinctive glass plaque at the Thai Dusit restaurant *(now called Salathip Thai)* in Market Street, Kingswinford. This was the former home of George

Woodall (arguably the greatest cameo engraver of the 19th century) and the occasion was the culmination of many months' work – mostly by Ian Dury of Stourbridge Glass Engravers but supported by the BGF – to install a commemorative plaque. This was duly done and, with Ian Dury officially unveiling it, the significant building had its historical status fittingly recognised.

Assembled guests included the restaurant owner Mr Guy Chanukal, Cllr Patrick Harley (Group Leader, Conservative Group DMBC); Cllr Natalie Neale (Kingswinford North and Wall Heath); Ian Dury (Stourbridge Glass Engravers and Project Coordinator); John Workman (Black Country Bugle) Chris Smith (Village Voice) and Mike Perkins (Amblecote History Society).

Winter Festival Weekend, 20th November - 1st December 2013
As part of the Festival held at Broadfield House Glass Museum, Allister Malcolm organised a competition for youngsters and visitors to blow the biggest bubble featuring one of his special works as a prize. Funds raised from this were split equally between the Friends of Broadfield House and the BGF.

Dudley Archives Centre
The new £6m Archives Centre was officially opened in January 2014. It is likely that many of our documents, letters, photographs and films will be stored at this brand new state-of-the-art facility.

Red by Night
The Black Country Living Museum's Red By Night event on 17th May 2014 was attended by glass artist and BGF Trustee Allister Malcolm who gave glassmaking demonstrations as well as handing out BGF leaflets and promoting the cause.

Red by Night glassmaking demonstrations

A Black Country Evening with Graham Fisher MBE
Graham Fisher was guest speaker at the Pedmore Sporting Club's Charity Dinner on 21st May 2014 at Stourbridge Golf Club where he spoke to local businessmen about Stourbridge glass, the proposed new museum and the 2012 Portland Vase Project. Pedmore Sporting Club is a local charity set up in 1970 and to date has given away over £1,260,000 to local worthy causes. Graham has addressed many similar events since and, along with Allister Malcolm, is seen at 'the public face' of BGF.

Celebrity Doodles Project, 2015
Following on from the World's Longest Glassmaking Demonstration, Allister Malcolm's Celebrity Doodle project raised £10,800 at the Fieldings Auction in October 2015. Doodles obtained from celebrities were used as a source of inspiration for artists to create a piece of glass. The finished works were auctioned at Fieldings Auctioneers Ltd.

Doodles were received from many celebrities including Steve Bull MBE (ex -Wolves and England footballer); Sir Trevor Brooking (ex-West Ham and England footballer); Sir Lenny Henry (comedian and actor); Frankie Valli (Four Seasons); Tony Hadley MBE (Spandau Ballet); Dame Emma Thompson (actress) and Raymond Blanc OBE (chef).

Robert Plant   Emma Thompson   Lenny Henry   Frankie Valli

The Heat is On

After more than five years of working alongside Dudley MBC, site owners Complex Development Projects Ltd and other interested parties, monies were secured via the European Regional Development Fund and the Heritage Lottery Fund (now National Lottery Heritage Fund) together with a degree of matched funding from BGF's own resources. Groundworks commenced in 2015 and in June 2016 the completion of the new White House Cone - museum of glass was marked by its first official event *The Heat is On.*

Organized by master glassmaker and BGF Trustee Allister Malcolm in association with Bruntnell-Astley, this inaugural showpiece marked the firing of the glassmaking furnace, the first such furnace here since the final days of Stuart Crystal, and celebrated the splendid new building as a focus for decades to come in helping promote the area's rich glass heritage and its practitioners whilst also acting as a beacon of excellence for the glass artisans of the future who are yet to emerge. White House Cone museum of glass was scheduled to be officially opened and fully operational commensurate with the Stourbridge Glass collection being transferred sometime mid-2017.

BGF continued to work closely with Dudley MBC in promoting the collection and on the wider stage of the glass world seeks to independently represent all other charities, glass organizations, glass artists and any others who have an interest in preserving, promoting and developing the glass heritage of Stourbridge and beyond.

'Radial Platter with gold leaf flecks and sapphire blue trailing', 45cm across, sold at auction in October 2016 for £300 with proceeds donated to the BGF.

Allister Malcolm, resident glassmaker at the new White House Cone museum of glass, Wordsley, working on the first piece of glass to be made on the old Stuart Crystal factory site since the glassworks closed in 2001. Dressed appropriately for such an auspicious occasion, Allister crafted the piece in front of a large crowd when the museum opened its doors for the first time with the *The Heat is On* exhibition in June 2016.

Other activities

Note: The best laid plans … etc.
The information reproduced below was as envisaged at the time. Although the Ruskin dig did take place there was no subsequent 'awareness campaign'. The plans are included here for context only.

The BGF in conjunction with Bryant Priest Newman, architects, were looking to arrange an awareness campaign in the local community to include open days, questionnaires and events. It was the intention to get local primary and secondary schools involved and perhaps look at a stained glass window project showing the story of the White House Cone and the different types of glass that were made in the Glass Quarter.

Following on from the awareness campaign there would be an excavation at the White House Cone site, similar to the one that was undertaken at Ruskin Glass Centre in May 2014. This would then be followed by the possible lighting of the ancient cone where it once stood after the site of the dig has been covered up. Press coverage for this would be huge and we could apply to the Arts Council for funding for this as well as Heritage Lottery and possibly also include a sculpture done by a local artist for the site.

It is hoped in the future to arrange a display at the British Museum in London with perhaps showing all three Portland Vases – the original one housed in the British Museum, the one from Corning and the 2012 Portland Vase, showcasing the importance of cameo glass.

Dr Paul Roberts contacted the BGF in June 2014 to offer to put on a small exhibition for the Charity and discussions are now taking place with Laura Philips at the British Museum.

The BGF sought other donations of contemporary, vintage and antique glass items for a major Fieldings glass auction in March 2016 which with the previously unsold pieces produced not only further income for the BGF but promotional exposure. The Charity would like to set up a free valuation service run by volunteers but where donations could be given to the Charity for this service if visitors wished to.

Preparatory groundworks commenced at the White House site in March 2013 where the remains of the original glass cone were uncovered. Hidden beneath what was once the looming figure of the cone lie the abandoned tunnels that would have been the source of air coming into the furnaces but also the route for bringing in coal to keep the fires burning and transporting new glass out for onwards transportation by canal. Regular tunnel tours are organised by the museum.

Donations received

On 15th October 2011 a cheque for £1,000 was presented by Barbara Beadman, Chair of The Friends of Broadfield House Glass Museum, to the BGF. The amount had been agreed by the Friends at their AGM as a gesture of support for the work of the BGF.

Donations received to date total £31,285.54 including Gift Aid. *(This figure has since increased substantially. Details of our major donors are listed in **GlassCuts** and on our website.)*

The day to day running costs of the Charity are mainly met from other sources meaning that almost £26,000 remains intact in our bank account to be used for the new museum.

British Soft Drinks Association gifts historic collection to BGF

The British Soft Drinks Association, the national body representing the collective interests of UK soft drinks manufacturers, gifted to the British Glass Foundation their collection of historic glass soda siphons and bottles.

The collection comprises about 20 soda siphons and 50 glass and ceramic bottles. Jill Ardagh, Director General of the British Soft Drinks Association in London, said *We are just about to move premises and sadly will no longer have room for our collection of historic glass soda siphons and bottles. I am very pleased that we have found a good home for the collection and it is heartening to know that the collection can find a new lease of life in both safe and appreciative hands.*

Following publicity regarding the collection the BGF was able to find a new, permanent home for the collection where the majority of it will be on display at the British Glass Manufacturers Confederation in their brand new foyer in Churchill Way, Sheffield. The surplus bottles were donated to the British Bottle Museum which is in the middle of a heritage centre at Elsecar.

The Kny Collection

The BGF has been offered six pieces from the near priceless Kny Collection. The collection was initially loaned to the BGF for the Dudley Archives Awareness Day. The owner then approached the BGF to ask if we would accept the collection for the new museum when it is built.

The Richard Golding Piece

Following the success of Allister Malcolm's Celebrity Doodles Project various glass artists were enlisted to create pieces inspired by the doodles. In March 2015 Richard Golding of Station Glass, Leicestershire, made such a piece in collaboration with Allister Malcolm based on the Frankie Valli doodle. All items were to be sold at auction by Fieldings Auctioneers Ltd of Stourbridge on 24th October 2015, with all proceeds to the British Glass Foundation.

  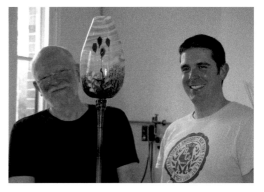

Heritage open week, September 2021

Our events supremo Louise is already hard at it compiling a list of forthcoming attractions at SGM; you can find out more by the 'Keeping in touch' panel or by staying tuned to *GlassCuts*, our website and our social media streams. In the meantime we give her and her colleagues Donna and Steven together with our volunteers a huge 'thank you' for their efforts throughout the recent Heritage Open Week held in late September and centring on the museum.

Louise reports on four tours of the museum that attracted a total of 49 visitors. For his part Graham Fisher was delighted to assist on the guided canal walks along 'The Crystal Canal' ending at SGM. Over two walks we entertained 53 visitors and attracted much positive feedback that makes us think this may not be a 'one-off' – it was to become a regular feature. Other events have been equally well supported; images are on our social media streams. Well done to all concerned.

The Allister Malcolm glass slipper, September 2021

At the time we introduced you to a delightful piece made by 'Our Allister' in his studio. It was a glass slipper, but for reasons of commercial confidentiality we could elaborate no further. The Organisation commissioning it applied rather strict sanctions on Al along the lines of *if you tell anyone we will have to send the boys round and eliminate you* and that was that. Until now.

We can now reveal, and are overjoyed to do so, that the Organisation was The Sony Corporation and the slipper is a central prop in their latest blockbuster, *Cinderella*, already the Number 1 film being streamed in the USA and by all accounts destined to be a worldwide cinematic sensation. Smack in the middle of it all is Allister's glass slipper. This is just a monster piece of news that, after more than 20 years at the coalface carving an already enviable international reputation, is likely to propel Allister Malcolm to worldwide recognition. On behalf of everyone associated with BGF and SGM we congratulate Allister to the rafters. If you would like to try and create your own glass slipper, watching him do it makes it look so simple. But that's only after a couple of decades of practise.

Exhibitions in the museum

Temporary exhibitions for our public opening and the early months thereafter featured:

Vanessa Cutler: *Journeys and Horizons* April – July 2022

Contemporary Glass Society at 25: *Past, Present, the Future* July – October 2022

Georgia Redpath: *Nature / Architecture* November 2022 – March 2023

Carnival Glass Society 40th Anniversary Exhibition April – November 2023

Georgia Redpath

Carnival Glass

Contemporary Glass Society (CGS) 25th Anniversary, 2022

Not surprisingly there was a lot going on in celebration, a major part of this being their collaboration with Stourbridge Glass Museum (SGM) in a rather special project, *viz*: *to commission a piece of contemporary glass to welcome and draw visitors into the Entrance Foyer area. This commissioned piece of work will be part of the Museum's permanent collection and will be installed and officially unveiled during the International Festival of Glass in August 2022.*

The aim of the work is not only to celebrate 25 years of the Contemporary Glass Society but also to stop visitors in their tracks with a work that dazzles and is thought provoking. It will be displayed in the entrance foyer of the new Museum to encourage visitors to explore the amazing glasswork on show at the Museum.

SB

Many interesting proposals were submitted and three were selected for further scrutiny and interviews. The artists shortlisted were Chris Day, Sacha Delabre and Anthony McCabe. It was a very hard decision between these three artists all of whose suggestions would have complemented the space. However, we were captivated by the storytelling and inclusive history of the UK (and in particular glassmaking in Stourbridge) that featured in one presentation.

The winner was Chris Day with his piece entitled *After the Darkness the Light* which is now on display in the upper gallery of the museum. Chris became a BGF Trustee in 2022.

Activities at the museum

Even before the official opening, the museum offered a variety of activities: opportunities to tour the new museum and experience the atmospheric tunnels that lie hidden beneath; talks exploring the museum's industrial heritage; walks around the glass quarter; and free workshops for people wanting to learn new skills with seasonal events such as Christmas wreath making and pumpkin carving.

As well as watching Allister and his team in the hotshop, visitors can also see glass engraver Thomas Southall and cameo artiste Terri-Louise Colledge at work, both being resident at the museum.

Tours of the new museum

Tunnel tours

Glass factories walking tours

Intaglio print making workshop

Willow stars workshop for children

Intuitive drawing workshop

From the hotshop

Time and again Allister comes up with stunning ideas to engage the public. From bauble making to hand casting sessions and sponsor plaques, initiatives also include the *World's Longest Glassmaking Demonstration* during the 2012 International Festival of Glass; the *Celebrity Doodles Project* providing inspiration for glass artists to create a piece of glass for auction; and *The Heat is On* exhibition to celebrate the opening of the museum. Such ventures raise considerable funds for BGF and the museum.

An exciting competition was launched where budding photographers and glass enthusiasts were set a challenge for when the studio opened to snap the best shot of 2022 in the hotshop, share it online (tagging us on social media), and be in with a chance to win a glassmaking experience.

Allister Malcolm (r) and his team; Darren Weed, Madeline Hughes, and Terri Malcolm

Museum Manager, Alex Goodger tries glassmaking

Supporters and sponsors

Our principal partners throughout the project were, and remain, **Complex Development Projects Ltd** (owners of the former Stuart site, which now comprises both the museum and unrelated retail holdings) and **Dudley MBC**, hitherto custodians of the Stourbridge Glass collection that was formerly displayed (in part) at Broadfield House Glass Museum that was also under the stewardship of Dudley MBC.

The demise of Broadfield House was the catalyst for the formation of the British Glass Foundation and its efforts to secure a new home for the collection. Detailed negotiations *inter alia* resulted in a leasing agreement with BGF on both the museum site and the glass collection, each for a period of 125 years.

It is with considerable gratitude we record that Mr Ian Harrabin MBE of Complex Development Projects Ltd has since most graciously offered to gift the museum site element to BGF. Arrangements for this transfer are currently in progress.

Higgs & Sons

This locally based firm of solicitors was engaged during the period when specialist advice was essential to the set up and operations of BGF as a charity. The BGF was given a special mention in their Yearbook 2012/13 *A Touch of Glass* where Kirsty McEwen, Associate, wrote *'Glass is a huge part of our local culture and we are lucky to have such a wonderful collection right here in the Midlands'.*

Clement Keys

The *Blue Basket* had been donated to the BGF by renowned glass artist Jaqueline Cooley and was originally offered at auction but failed to sell. That's when Clement Keys stepped up to the mark agreeing to purchase the piece. Simon Atkins, Partner at Clement Keys, said: *'The Blue Basket is a truly beautiful piece that will add an extra dimension of depth and quality to our premises from the moment it goes on display. We have been delighted to have worked with the BGF in its start-up phase and have assisted the Trustees with the establishment of the Charity, the setting up of a gift-aid scheme as well as providing training in the area of finance and accounts. We fully support the work of BGF and wish them every success in working with Dudley Council to achieve the best for the glass collections'.*

Simon Atkins with Jaqueline Cooley
'Blue Basket - fused and slumped woven blue bowl'
48cm across, 7cm tall

Arrangements were made for a formal presentation at Broadfield House Glass Museum on 7th November 2011.

A project of this magnitude has necessitated the involvement of numerous advisors, consultants and contractors along the way, the majority of whom are based local to, or a short geographical distance from, the new museum. This was a deliberate policy by BGF in order to strengthen the museum's ties to the community.

The principal contributors

Gavin Whitehouse, formerly of Clement Keys, opened his own practice **Bennett Whitehouse** based at Brierley Hill, and joined BGF as our Accountant and Trustee.

JLA Consulting advised us in the early stages of fundraising

Bryant Priest Newman of Birmingham prepared early artists' impressions and were the original architects employed by Complex Development Projects Ltd. We are grateful to Dean Shaw for his assistance with forecourt landscaping and to Larry Priest who is now a BGF Trustee.

Demolition work on the site in preparation for refurbishment was by **Humphries Demolition Ltd**, Wednesbury. Building work was by **Croft Building & Conservation Ltd** of Cannock.

Design Consultants **The Hub** of Redditch were the main contractors for the internal fit-out, subcontracting to **Armour** (glass display cabinets) and **Spiral** (digital interactive displays).

Daniel Sutton of **DesignMap** London Ltd provided the internal design.

PMP Consultants Ltd of Birmingham were our Quantity Surveyors and Contract Administrators for the development and fit-out of new exhibition space.

Jack Moody Ltd of Wolverhampton carried out the frontal landscaping; **Simworx** of Kingswinford fitted the unique lighting structure.

Born Communication Ltd based in Wolverhampton, now in Hackney were our web designers.

Wondrous Ltd of Wordsley were our PR company up to and for a short time after the museum was officially opened by HRH The Duke of Gloucester in April 2023.

Serveline IT Ltd of Kinver handle our IT, servers and telephones.

Ian Watt of **E L Electrics**, Hagley carried out our electrical work including wiring the hot glass studio.

Jacqui Watson of Wall Heath has been consistently supportive in our funding advice and bids.

Brierley Printers Ltd of Stourbridge print our leaflets, museum foamex boards and so forth.

Evaluation Consultant **Oliver Carrington**, based in Portugal but with connections to the area, is tasked with reporting back to National Lottery Heritage Fund at the completion of the project.

Harris Lamb of Birmingham are managing agents for the rental units.

The British Glass Foundation would like to thank the following organisations for their financial contributions and moral support:

National Lottery Heritage Fund	Scottish Glass Society
European Regional Development Fund	Enovert Community Trust
Complex Development Projects Ltd	Ibstock Enovert Trust
Friends of Broadfield House Glass Museum	Garfield Weston Foundation
The Glass Association :: The Glass Circle	Richardson Brothers Charity Foundation
The Contemporary Glass Society	Owen Family Trust
University of Wolverhampton	The Grimmitt Trust
The Guild of Glass Engravers	The Rowlands Trust
British Glass	The Edward Cadbury Charitable Trust
Glass Manufacturers Federation Education Trust	William A Cadbury Charitable Trust
Fieldings Auctioneers Ltd	GNC Trust
John Ellerman Foundation	The Charles Hayward Foundation
The Clive Richards Foundation	The Pilgrim Trust
The Headley Trust	The FCC Communities Foundation

Many thanks also to all supporters, volunteers, local businesses and glass artists without whom the new museum would not be possible, with apologies to anyone we may have inadvertently omitted.

Ruin to rebirth

Dereliction

The Stuart Crystal factory site had lain unused since its closure in 2001. Subject to vandalism, set on fire and generally abused, the site was in a sorry state when proposals were made to build the new museum there.

Design proposals

As part of the application for funding, architects Bryant Priest Newman submitted plans for the new museum together with suggested layouts for the exhibits on upper and lower galleries. An open courtyard was planned, featuring a light structure to mark the location of the original Stuart Crystal glass cone – an element later to be incorporated into the landscaping.

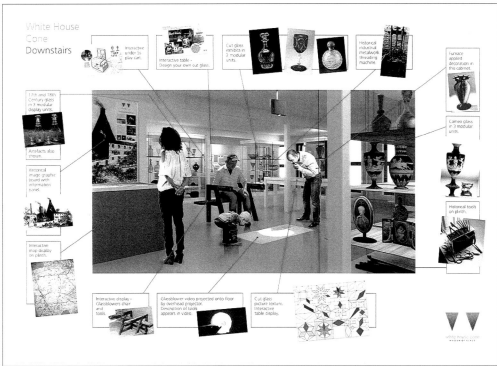

Demolition

Work by Humphries Demolition Ltd began in earnest in February 2015 with the clearance of the derelict site and stabilisation work to the fire-damaged elements of the Grade II listed building. The timing was propitious; BGF had been advised that just one more fire or one more harsh winter and the structure would have been damaged beyond recovery.

Construction begins

By May, work by Croft Building & Conservation Ltd was underway. The scheme was to comprise the glass museum housed in the Newhouse Building at the entrance to the site and the conversion of the Mill Buildings to the rear to provide commercial units as well as 18 residential apartments above. A separate development of 49 homes was planned along the canalside adjacent to the site.

Work in progress

By the end of September 2015 both the interior fabric and exterior shell were attracting visits from supporters and sponsors to view progress and discuss final appearance.

Coming along nicely

Progress from here was rapid and by November 2015 a key element, the Hot Studio, was ready to accept equipment. By Spring 2016 the exterior of the museum was recognisable in its near-completed form.

Internal fit-out

The fit-out work at the new museum commenced on 4th January 2022 and completed by 25th February. Design Consultants The Hub of Worcestershire were the main contractors, subcontracting to Armour for the glass display cabinets and Spiral for the digital interactive displays.

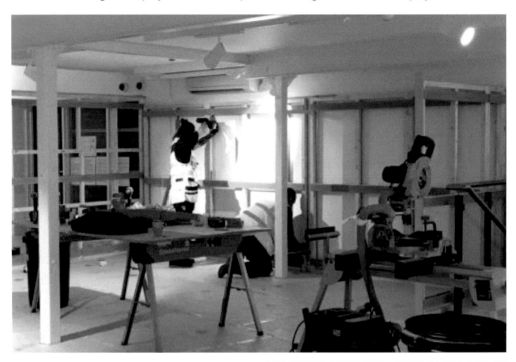

Filling the cabinets

The glass items were moved into the new cabinets in March 2022. By definition, the museum's focus had to be on the Stourbridge Glass collection but not at the expense of excluding exceptional though unrelated acquisitions: a piece by renowned studio artist Dale Chihuly of the USA is in the upstairs gallery and there are numerous other hugely significant examples on display.

Displays

The two floors in the main exhibition area are packed with a range of exhibits from various periods, together with display boards outlining their context and history. There are also interactive displays and hands-on activities. Available space is utilised to the maximum extent that presentation and accessibility permits. Even so, the Stourbridge Glass collection alone is so comprehensive that only a small fraction can be shown at any given time. The intention is to rotate pieces with others held in safe storage elsewhere.

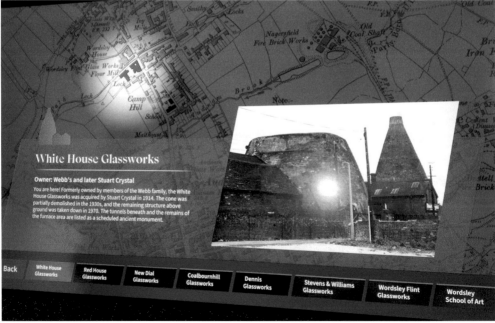

Landscaping

Following the initial landscaping work in 2017 funded by Cory Environmental Trust In Britain and Ibstock Cory Environmental Trust (now both known as Enovert Community Trust) the final stage was funded by FCC Communities Foundation in 2023. The work was carried out by Jack Moody Landscaping & Civil Engineering Ltd of Wolverhampton greatly enhancing the museum forecourt. The spectacular lighting structure denoting the site of the original White House glass cone was custom-built and installed by Simworx of Kingswinford.

The finishing touch

In *GlassCuts 176* (dated 17.3.21) we told the tale of a wonderful relic that was saved from being dumped in a skip and lost forever by the fortunate intervention of our resident glassmaker. At the time our plan was to conserve the old Stuart Crystal enamelled sign, for that is what it was, so that at some stage it could be mounted in the entrance area of the museum as a nod to the building's former role as a major glass factory.

We engaged a metal conservator to clean the sign but to keep the weathered patina as an indication of its age and heritage. In the meantime we appealed to anyone who could assist us in restoring it to some semblance of its former self in better times. Old enamelled signs are always an attraction and at almost five metres long this one is a whopper.

But then events moved on apace and a short time later we were delighted to announce that the Trustees of The Worshipful Company of Glass Sellers of London Charity Fund offered to finance the cost of refurbishment, thereby not only helping preserve the sign for posterity but also providing a fitting feature for visitors to this iconic site.

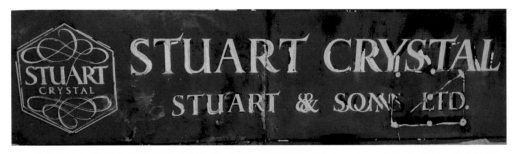

Onwards and upwards

Drawing it together
The purpose of this book, as described in the introduction, is to relate and preserve for posterity the story of some thirteen years between the formation of the British Glass Foundation and its crowning achievement in opening Stourbridge Glass Museum. So, here it is; job done.

However, it would be remiss not to venture beyond the museum's opening and to bring its remarkable narrative up to date as at publication of this work in late 2023, if only to note how post-opening occurrences have quickly gained momentum.

For this synopsis I have therefore referred to events as recorded in the BGF's email bulletin *GlassCuts* since the museum's 'soft' opening on 9th April 2022 (from issue 201 dated 18.4.22 onwards). The list is not exhaustive though sufficient is alluded to here to indicate the scope. Further details of these and more can be found in *GlassCuts*, all issues of which are archived chronologically on the British Glass Foundation and Stourbridge Glass Museum websites.

They are in no particular order, other than I consider the last three notices *(The official opening*; *Change of power; And finally ...)* to be those of the greatest moment.

The teams; BGF and SGM
The BGF Trustees are supported by Advisors and Ambassadors holding specialist skills, subject to ongoing review and with several notable additions since the Charity's formation. These are recorded herein on pages 12-13.

BGF Trading
Directors are: Graham Knowles, Gavin Whitehouse, Alexander Goodger and Leigh White.
This is the trading arm for the Charity through which all bills and salaries are paid. Event, ticket and shop sales also go through the trading company as well as the rental income. Any profit at the end of each financial year is passed to the Charity.

The SGM team
Stourbridge Glass Museum now enjoys a full complement of professionals administering the site, aided by a cohesive volunteer base, which affords the opportunity for the BGF Trustees to focus on their role of Governance moreso than their earlier role of being almost exclusively hands-on.

Alexander Goodger MA: Museum Manager

Alexander holds a BA in History plus an MA (merit) in Heritage Management. He took up his position as Stourbridge Glass Museum Manager on 4th October 2022, having previously been Manager at Dundee Museum of Transport (No.1 on Trip Advisor for Things To Do In Dundee) and has almost a decade of management and heritage experience including two years as Manager & Curator at Nantwich Museum. At Dundee Museum, Alexander managed six staff and more than forty volunteers to support the creation of the world's first carbon-neutral transport museum. He has assisted SGM in becoming No.1 on Tripadvisor for Things To Do In Stourbridge. Alexander is also a Director of BGF Trading, the commercial arm of the Charity.

Harrison Davies MA: Curator and Projects Officer

Harrison holds a BA (Hons) in Archaeology & Ancient History and an MA in Conservation of the Historic Environment. He assumed his role on 26th April 2022 and is responsible for safeguarding the Stourbridge Glass Collection. He was a key player in Stourbridge Glass Museum obtaining its coveted Accreditation in July 2023. He has a particular interest in Black Country and Birmingham heritage, having worked professionally and as a volunteer in many local museums both front-of-house, delivering events, and in collections care. Most recently he was Collections Inventory Assistant for Birmingham Museums Trust, working on Birmingham Museum and Art Gallery's historical collections and artworks, including glass.

Corrina Field: Events & Education Coordinator

Corrina was formerly a Teaching Assistant at Ridgewood High School in Stourbridge before taking up her role at the Museum on 4th October 2022. She is also a glass artist and has attended the International Festival of Glass where she has given talks on her own work. She attended University of Wolverhampton where she obtained a BA (Hons) in 3D Glass Design followed by a Master's Degree in Applied Arts: Glass. Corrina has already arranged numerous events at Stourbridge Glass Museum, at times working closely with our colleagues at the Canal & River Trust, and has helped enormously in embedding the museum as an integral part of the local heritage and activity scene.

Moemi Madigan: Volunteer Coordinator

Moemi ('Mo') Madigan took up the role of Volunteer Coordinator on 2nd August 2022. Born in Japan, Mo is a self-employed translator/interpreter and a qualified Blue Badge Tourist Guide in the Japanese language for Heart of England. Moemi is responsible for a team of volunteers, currently numbering around 60, in various roles that are essential to run the museum. She is also responsible for the Museum shop.

Lynn Boleyn MBE: Business Manager and Secretary

Lynn undertakes much of the background work that oils the cogs at BGF including minutes of meetings, general correspondence and all the other unsung but essential duties that help keep the organisation on an even keel. She also works alongside the author in producing *GlassCuts* by way of layout and insertion of imagery before then distributing the bulletin across an ever-expanding database. She is Business Manager at SGM and personal Secretary to BGF Chairman Graham Knowles. Away from BGF and SGM Lynn is a former local councillor who is now notably a Charity Trustee of Kewford Eagles Football Club in Wall Heath, near Stourbridge. In 2015 she was awarded an MBE for Services to the Community of Wall Heath.

Volunteers

The Stourbridge Glass Museum volunteer group has established an enviable reputation for enhancing the quality of the museum and its learning experience for all ages. A particular favourite is the museum Tunnel Tours exploring the connecting passages beneath the site, but these enthusiastic stalwarts also undertake many other public-facing roles and are a vital component in the first line of welcome to the People's Museum.

SGM volunteer, Moemi Madigan (left), Harrison Davies and Alex Goodger (right) with delegates representing the National Museum of South Korea, researching glass housed in their Royal Palaces Collection

SGM volunteers, left to right:
Ivet Benova; Eileen Sanders; Shirley Parker; Heather Shotton; Antonia Barnsley and Roy Cartwright

Founding Patrons scheme

A subscription-based museum Patronage in return for benefits-in-kind is aimed at the seriously committed glass enthusiast. Founding Patrons help to both secure the museum's sustainability and support us at this time of exceptional challenge and opportunity. Current Patrons are;

Dame Jenifer Wilson-Barnett	Giles Woodward
Viv Astling OBE	David Williams-Thomas DL
John H Hughes	Graham Knowles
Clive Manison	Gavin Whitehouse

A separate Membership Scheme is under consideration.

Informal *ad hoc* information service

This grew like topsy out of nothing more than attempting to answer readers' queries about their favourite pieces of glass. These are either resolved in-house or put out to the *GlassCuts* readership. Our success rate is rewardingly high.

Contemporary reportage

From modest beginnings with Issue 1 released on 20th October 2011, *GlassCuts* has become both the definitive 'Journal of the BGF' and 'the voice of SGM', attracting correspondence from all over the world including Eastern Europe, USA, Canada, Australia, the Solomon Islands and Trinidad & Tobago.

Promotion of artists and events

In pursuit of our acceptance as an umbrella organisation for the wider glass world we are now high on the lists of many individuals and organisations who choose to further the news of their endeavours through our offices.

Student liaison and placements

Our educational facilities now include resource access and, working in conjunction with external organisations, placement facilities for students and researchers.

Exhibitions and festivals

Stourbridge Glass Museum has already proved its efficacy in staging a wide variety of shows, events and presentations; this can only increase for the better.

The biennial International Festival of Glass will be held for the last time in Stourbridge and handed over to new custodians at the end of the 10th International Festival of Glass, 23rd - 26th August 2024. These are early days but as at the time of the announcement BGF and SGM are already considering proposals as to how they may take a positive role in continuing to promote Stourbridge Glass and its practitioners; very much a case of 'watch this space'.

Awards

The museum has accrued several awards but arguably the most prestigious to date is the *Tripadvisor Awards 2023 Travellers' Choice*. This speaks volumes about our staff and volunteers.

In August 2023 an application was submitted to the Tiqets Remarkable Venue Awards Best Hidden Gem, an international accolade celebrating the best museums and attractions in the world. Simply to be considered is an achievement.

Ongoing activities

Upon opening, in order to entertain, inform, educate and engage with our audience, Stourbridge Glass Museum immediately initiated a comprehensive programme of activities including educational programmes, hands-on experiences, demonstrations, tours and presentations that already number in their hundreds. This is expected to develop and expand; full details are broadcast via local and social media, email communications and our website.

Acquisitions

The museum has an acquisitions policy and in addition to receiving bequests and donations, monitors outlets for impending sales and auctions that may be of interest. We are pleased to enjoy the services of BGF Trustee Will Farmer, Fieldings Auctioneers Ltd, Stourbridge, who is eminently qualified to advise on such matters. Recent acquisitions of significance have included various artefacts and tools of cameo engraver George Woodall, the Letters Patent of glass magnate Benjamin Richardson, diverse items of glassware and a collation of historical documents pertaining to Whitefriars Glass.

Museum Curator, Harrison Davies examines the Benjamin Richardson Letters Patent

Giving back

The BGF has secured a sponsorship package with Dudley Town Football Club (DTFC) in the same style as our existing arrangement with Penn Colts that will include the Stourbridge Glass Museum logo on the shirts worn by the players on each match day, a prominent banner at the ground and diverse social media coverage. Graham Knowles, Chairman of BGF, said: *We are delighted to have secured this deal which is indicative of our wish to reciprocate the support that has been given to us throughout the local community.*

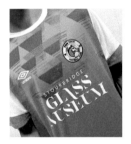

Showing the way

A sign has been installed on the waterside frontage of the museum adjacent to Glasshouse Bridge, which means that thousands of drivers and passers-by in both directions along the A491 at Wordsley (and indeed the Stourbridge Canal for that matter) can now see exactly where we are. Nice one.

The official opening

The museum was due to open to the public in April 2022 followed by an official opening in September of that year. Plans were stymied by the sad death of Queen Elizabeth II on 8th September 2022 when her representative, HRH The Duke of Gloucester, then became engaged with affairs of State. He subsequently honoured his commitment and graciously performed the official opening of Stourbridge Glass Museum on 19th April 2023, almost exactly one year to the day after originally planned. Graham Knowles invited HRH to sign a glass plaque donated and specially made for the occasion by Allister Malcolm, resident glassmaker, and engraved by Terri-Louise Colledge, resident cameo glass engraver.

Change of power

Never a man to rest on his laurels, SGM resident glassmaker and fellow Trustee Allister Malcolm, became increasingly concerned for his power supply, not least its security and the cost thereof, following well-documented developments in Ukraine and worldwide upsets to markets including gas and other fuel. Allister attacked the problem head-on by doing a complete re-evaluation of his vital furnace and gloryhole equipment, concluding the best way forward was via electricity.

In July 2023 Allister announced he would be taking a new concept, the 'EGO' (electric gloryhole/ reheating chamber) for a 'test drive' over the coming months. He was quoted: *We are looking forward to seeing how it performs and are working closely with Interpower Induction UK in developing it. As it's the first of its kind we have our fingers crossed that it represents the future of studio glassmaking.*

By sheer coincidence, and clearly indicating that Allister – and, in turn, Stourbridge Glass Museum – is already ahead of the curve, came news of the official opening of the Glass Futures Global Centre of Excellence, a £54m venture in St Helens soon be home to a unique experimental furnace and other technology that will pioneer ways of making carbon-neutral glass.

Immediately prior to us going to press Allister informs us that initial calculations indicate a considerable increase in fuel efficiency, with a corresponding decrease in costs and carbon footprint. With the full support of BGF, Allister has invested a great deal of time and an equal amount of finance in choosing to go electric in his furnace, gloryhole and cooling lehr, all accompanied by solar panels on the roof that will benefit not only the glassmaking side of the museum's operations but the museum itself. Having now operated under these new conditions for sufficiently long to obtain viable data, he has since been calculating, extrapolating, interpolating and crunching every bit of information and then subjected it all to independent rigour before declaring his findings. And the results across the board are impressive.

Allister in his hotshop surrounded by new 'green' glassmaking technology

And finally ...
From *You'll never do it* to full accreditation

In August 2023 it was announced that Stourbridge Glass Museum had been awarded the coveted **Full Accreditation Status**. This is the Gold Standard of recognition and elevates SGM to the very highest echelons, setting the museum squarely amongst the major players of the museum world. Our news release said it all:

Stourbridge Glass Museum is a museum dedicated to the history of glassmaking. The museum aims to preserve the heritage of glassmaking and promote understanding, appreciation, and enjoyment of glass to a diverse range of audiences. It also offers visitors an opportunity to observe contemporary glass artists in action, participate in hands-on workshops, and purchase unique glassware from their shop. The Museum provides an excellent insight into the rich history and craftsmanship of glassmaking in the region.

Administered by Arts Council England on behalf of the UK Accreditation Partnership, Accreditation is the benchmark for well-run Museums and Galleries.

The new accreditation status means that Stourbridge Glass Museum is properly managed and governed to the nationally agreed industry standard and shows the museum takes proper care of its collections, sharing them with visitors and keeping them safe for future generations'.

Accreditation opens exciting funding opportunities, allows museums to host touring exhibitions and gives access to professional advice and support. It also gives confidence to donors and sponsors who may wish to support the museum in preserving heritage and inspiring future generations.

Epilogue

So, was it worth the effort? Did we accomplish that which we set out to attain? How was success measured and then realised? Well, there's no magic formula. But perhaps this comes close ...

The only thing that makes a dream impossible to achieve is the fear of failure
Paulo Coelho De Souza, novelist.

Giving up was not a realistic option. Neither did we seriously consider failure. And as for those assertions of *You'll never do it* (pg 8), well, perhaps the defence can now rest its case.

Thanks to all who gave us faith and helped us see beyond the horizon.